JOURNEY
to
JOY

Robert J. Werberig

CONCORDIA PUBLISHING HOUSE
ST. LOUIS   LONDON

Concordia Publishing House, St. Louis, Missouri
Concordia Publishing House Ltd., London, E. C. 1
Copyright © 1971 by Concordia Publishing House
Library of Congress Catalog Card No. 72-153648
ISBN-0-570-06382-5

MANUFACTURED IN THE UNITED STATES OF AMERICA

Contents

JOURNEY
to
JOY

Unity

That they all may be one; as Thou, Father, art in Me, and I in Thee, that they also may be one in Us; that the world may believe that Thou hast sent Me.

John 17:21

Everyone knows about the noise, activity, and anxiety of life today. We are surrounded by its threats and uncertainties, its wearying demands, and its unrelenting clamor for our time, our participation, our involvement.

And so we frequently think these days, with some wistfulness, about how great it would be if we could only find time to sit back to think about what's happening and how we're turning out after all these years — and then maybe to discover again our resources of courage and endurance as Christians before returning to the running, working, and scheduling again.

Perhaps they never really knew it, but the people of the church of the distant past were actually reaching forward to bless us when they inaugurated the season of Lent as part of the church year. Because Lent is just such a time: a time for retreat and temporary withdrawal, a time for sinking deeper roots into the ground of meaning, a time for recharging the batteries of life.

This Lent we propose to go on a journey — a journey to Joy. People who come back from trips abroad say that travel broadens one's perspectives on life. They report that in their encounters with different cultures and different people their insights are deepened, expanded, sharpened. Some even say that their whole appraisal of life and meaning and truth and outlook are definitely changed. Well, this Lent *our* journey will take us along some special paths that are close to the heart of God. I can say this because our journey will move, point by point, through the High-Priestly prayer of God's own Son — the prayer that filled His last occasion of intimate communion with His Father before He went to Gethsemane and the cross.

This prayer of Jesus is significant because it sums up, in the face of impending death, a concentration of the Savior's deepest desires for what He thinks the effects of His work should be. It is significant, furthermore, because all of what He prays for is what He thinks we should have — what He wants for us, His people.

Tonight, as we approach the first milestone on the way, we learn that His first petition to the Father is for our unity, our oneness. Listen to Him:

"That they all may be one; as Thou, Father, art in Me, and I in Thee, that they also may be one in Us; that the world may believe that Thou hast sent Me."

Wherever God is — and that is everywhere — there are signs of unity, of connectedness, of contact and relationship. In the total design of the world, as well as in that of all its parts, we see reflections of the way He wants us to be. We marvel at the incredible interlocking systems of forces in our huge solar system, at the balances of contained and active energies that preserve its order, process, and life. We know about the intricate and delicate interrelations of the "environmental web," about the purpose behind the seasonal pulse and alternation of productivity and rest. We think about the whole range of functional balances within the multiplicity of coordinated physiological systems constantly going on in our own bodies. In all of these we sense something of not only the way *God* is but also the way He would have *us* be. For the principles are always there — connection, interrelation, and the communication of power or energy across the points of juncture in relationships. So does the branch relate to the vine. So does God desire that we be related *to Him* and *to one another;* that we be in mutual connection, in relationship; that there be unity.

8

Jesus prayed for the unity of His people, the church. And God answered that prayer. For whether we know it, sense it, see it, affirm it, or not, in Christ all of us are united in one Lord, one faith, one Baptism with one God and Father of us all. For despite all surface appearances to the contrary, we are united in terms of our common relationship with God *in Christ;* and under His lordship, with one another, under God, we are called into a real mutuality for the maintenance of godly service toward one another through the communication of strength from faith to faith and through the active witness of our love. And that purpose of our relatedness moves on. For where the church begins to sense within its body the unifying dynamics of the presence of Christ, there too will it be surprised by the happy realization of a profound potential in its midst. It will sense *its* role as a point of juncture across which power can be communicated to its own membership and the world, and it will prize and cherish its unity as prerequisite to fulfilling its task of bearing witness to the world. For unity in the church is the prelude of its mission. For this the Lord of the church prays when He says: "That they also may be one in Us; that the world may believe that Thou hast sent Me."

"God will have all men to be saved and to come unto the knowledge of the truth." His love extends to all men everywhere. And that men may see the good works of Christians and glorify the Father through faith in His Son, the lived-out truth of the church's oneness needs to be demonstrated. For unity in the church is a prerequisite of mission.

We that are here tonight are a living symbol of this oneness. We are united in our *diversity.* We are men and women, children and adults. A worker earning $6,000 a year could be next to an executive earning $50,000 a year. There are smart people and not-so-smart people, gifted and unskilled, good-looking and plain, unhappy and happy, ailing and healthy, fragile and strong — all of us made up of individual pluses and minuses, of unique weaknesses and unique strengths. Nobody is the same as anyone else. Yet all are one in Christ.

And it is this interesting quality of diversity that forms the basis of our need for one another. We are designed by our make-up to share — to communicate — across the contact points of our relationships with one another. For we *do* need one another, and our individual differences become the *opportunity* for that sharing to go on which fills the needs existing among us from man to man. The weak man needs the strength of the strong. The poor man needs the wealth of the rich. The sorrowful man needs the ministry of the joyful one. And the sick need the care of the healthy and the whole. Farmers have always needed builders, and builders have always needed farmers. The child has always needed the direct and firm practicality of the father. And it has always also needed the emotional, subjective tenderness of the mother.

Our mutual interdependence, and the movements of ministry toward need that happens within relationships, not only guarantees growth and maturity for the church but is also the practical basis for a unity that reflects the love of Christ to the world. For when the world sees this ministry at work among the members of a congregation, it observes with a stimulated curiosity, "See how they *love* one another!" When the corporate image of a congregation begins to mirror the attitudes and actions of Jesus Christ as He is known through the Gospel, then that congregation has already embarked on the mission of making all men one with the Father and the Son.

Sounds pretty idealistic, I admit. We are perhaps more impressed with our insulation from one another, with relational breakdowns and polarizations. Our families — and even this congregational family — reflect a considerable number of relational weaknesses and even breaks. Old grudges and fixed impressions, real and imagined, have turned "points of contact" into walls that separate: gaps between generations, differing economic and political groupings, lack of sensitivity, the will to dominate, and so on. The very differences that form the basis for our mutual service and unity become the basis for making *separating* comparisons. And where the points of juncture and contact separate, it's like "pulling out the plug" on mutual ministry, which pulls out the plug on the church's unity, which results in a power failure that seriously affects our ministry to the world. For the unbelieving man then has no true image of the Christ through whom the church is commissioned to call him into the unity of the Father and the Son. And when it comes to functional relations of ministry in a congregation, it is vital for the congregation's unity and mission that its members be "hanging *in* there," and not "hung up."

Jesus' prayer to His Father implied a total obedience to the carrying out of His Father's will. And He knew that this meant His own death. This was clear, for in the Father's plan, Jesus Himself was sent to be the point of juncture and contact between the Father and the fallen world. The oneness for which Jesus prayed could be worked out only by One who would function as connecting point for a relationship across which power, in the form of the life of God, could flow. And so God hammered the plus of His cross into the ground of the world, permitting His Son to die. Christ's death broke the bondage of man's sinfulness and freed him to plug into the power of God through faith. That's why Christ's death and resurrection are called an atonement — because they have taken away the barriers that separated man from God and made the way open for a dynamic ministry-relationship between God and man.

When it was all over, Jesus turned to His disciples and said, "As the Father hath sent Me, even so send I you." He says this to the church; and therewith He expects us to occupy the same position between God and the world as He once did: as communicators, interpreters; as juncture — point and power — transmitter between Him and people everywhere; as suffering servants; as people who atone, who heal, who struggle in the gaps to bring together

11

need and supply, who live as an enabling group in the middle ground between unreconciled people, who live in the sacrificial tradition of that great Man-in-the-Middle, Jesus Christ.

God is One who is known by His work of "setting the solitary into families," who unites and empowers for ministry. You need proof? See His Word as it lives in people by His power in it and them. See His uniting Supper, where through the body and blood of His Son as point of juncture He communicates His love, life, and power to His people. See your place and purpose in His communion of saints — and that communion as His place of relationship with a lost world, which He so deeply loves. And you can almost hear *yourself* praying:

"That they all may be one; as Thou, Father, art in me, and I in Thee, that they also may be one in us; that the world may believe that Thou hast sent me."

Glorify

All Mine are Thine, and Thine are Mine, and I am glorified in them.
John 17:10

Someone has said that all of life — all creation, all of history and mankind — are like the elements of a tremendous offering in the process of being consecrated. It's as if we and all things were caught up in that moment in which the High Priest elevates the priceless gift before the King and then lays it at His feet — the supreme and ultimate act of giving glory to the Most High God.

To make such an offering has always been the privilege and function of the High Priest alone. And it is at this point in His High-Priestly work that we encounter Jesus tonight — at the second milestone of our Lenten "Journey to Joy." Jesus Christ, our High Priest, is about to accomplish the supreme work of readying and offering up *a people* to His Father. He has gathered into a body a unique, consecrated people, who in a real sense are the products of His love and labor and life, to present them as a gift to His Father. As He does so, He utters words that express both the basis for this high act of worship and its meaning for Himself:

"All Mine are Thine, and Thine are Mine, and I am glorified in them."

Since the beginnings of human history the prestige, importance, and worth of men has been measured largely in terms of the amount and quality of their possessions. The tombs, monuments, and written records of the ancient kings and dignitaries of the past are filled with lengthy accounts of their glories — the lands they controlled and conquered, their treasures of precious stones and metals, the products of their national industries and military plunders, the size of their households, their slave and cattle holdings, and so on. Their reputations and esteem as kings depended on the abundance of their wealth, for that was their glory. That was what glorified them.

In a sense the same holds true today. People rate themselves (and are rated by others) pretty much on the basis of the quantity and quality of their possessions. Our possessions are our glory too. We are glorified, or derive a sense of our own worth from the things we own — from the years of input that result in a home, a car, a family of growing children, a reputation we have, or a position we hold. And such "objects" are not only the products of some of the deepest desires and loves of our hearts but are also the things toward which and for which we devote most of our time, our effort, and our labor. In short, what I choose to own — what I seek with fervor, effort, and determination — whatever I deliver up my life for — that is my glory. And when I gather together the fruits of all my longing, labor, and the pursuits of a lifetime, what that all adds up to *glorifies* me. It bears witness to the set and nature of my true self. It publicizes, for anyone to see, what my living has really meant — indeed, why I lived at all.

Similarly, people evaluate us *through* our possessions, whether they be things, elements of our character, our words, or forms of our behavior. People tend to make judgments about us on the basis of what we wear or what we drive, or the length of our hair, or whether or not we wear a beard. They observe our children and draw inferences about our home life. They decide things about us as people on the basis of what we create, manufacture, produce — in short, what "surfaces," what we offer from out of the centers and sources of our persons. And it is on the basis of these that we are "made public," "known," "evaluated." For we are also *glorified* by what we present and shed of ourselves into the world's life.

God too is glorified by all the things that point to His essential character. Look at all that He has made. See the abundance, intricacy, and unquenchable wisdom of His creation. Marvel at its profound design and its limitless dimensions, its timing and the incomparable providence that preserves the life that it contains. And behold the crown of it all — the human being! The very goodness of creation is a reflection of the basic goodness of God Himself and supports our guesswork as to what He's really like.

With so much to glorify Him, God must indeed be proud. Bue He's not. At least not entirely.

Have you ever been misrepresented? Have you ever said something, done something that began in completely "good faith" and with the best of intentions but was suddenly turned into something negative, destructive, and completely foreign to your original interpretation and intent? Have you ever been innocently accused of something, and even when the accusation was totally untrue, noticed the decline in your relationships with people as the news got around: how normal reactions changed, how people tended to avoid you, and how virtually helpless you were to change or break the rumor? Innocently and not, many people suffer untold damage, hardship, and unhappiness simply by virtue of their being misrepresented, misinterpreted, misunderstood. And in many instances what they perceived to be their glory became in fact their shame.

So it is with God. Mankiñd, prize of His creation, made to be a little lower than the angels, became God's deepest problem. The men who bore God's image and resemblance betrayed and sullied it and simultaneously broadcast a deceptive caricature of what their God was like. How could they thus be His "glory"? How could they glorify Him when their lives and allegiances smothered the evidences of His goodness, His changeless love, His gracious provision? Man was God's problem. For as he lived, produced, expressed, responded, and influenced, man fell short of glorifying God as He really and always is. And because the glory of man became divorced from the glory of God, man could only descend

17

to the glorification of himself. And that kind of glorying, subject to the distortions of man's fallenness and sin, could only say *the wrong things* about God's authentic personality and being.

And so it is clear: God could never receive as His glory an offering that did not reflect Him in truth, that did not bear the marks and characteristics of a people who came forth from the sources and centers of His own person.

Even Christians are not immune. We participate in a misrepresentation of God. For it is one of the native and persistent characteristics of men that they seek to glorify themselves. We pile up and beautify, cultivate and adorn our children, our homes, our belongings. We *use* them in our elbowing for esteem, in an attempt to receive glory, to be glorified by them. We anchor their meaning for our lives and for ourselves exclusively within ourselves, ignoring that they all indeed belong to *God*. Vocationally, socially, educationally, financially, even ecclesiastically, we tend to look back across a clutter of accomplishments with self-congratulation, priding ourselves on our self-defined "progress," crediting every good and grace and blessing to our prowess, power, capability, endurance, and intelligent management. Such an outlook and estimate of life robs God. And its self-inflation and exclusivism clearly misrepresent to the world the truth about a God whose nature abounds with an outgoing, long-suffering, sacrificial, and enduring love.

The first sins ever committed by man, recorded in the early chapters of Genesis, demonstrate the eager readiness with which man seeks to make of himself the beginning and end of all things, and his obstinate striving to use all things toward achieving that end. How then can Christ offer up to His Father a people who do not glorify Him but rather seek to clutch and use His wealth — His glory — as if it were exclusively their own? How can God accept such people as an offering?

How can God accept even us, gathered here tonight, a people who *know* what His will is for us and all men, yet constantly misrepresent Him by the deficient quality and quantity of lives that are *supposed* to be rooted in Him? How can He receive even us, who in fact *take for ourselves* what God intended for us to *use* in His universal and saving purpose and mission? The answer is simple. It is the only answer: He accepts us in Christ.

This is a profound and far-reaching truth. For when Jesus as God's High Priest offered up the family of God to His Father, He did so in anticipation of His own suffering and death. It would be *for* that family. It would be *for* all those whom God had given Him. Jesus was lifted up, so that after He drew all men to Himself, He could offer up a people: all those who believed in Him and to whom He gave power to become the sons of God, a people born again, not out of the human origins of human flesh or human striving but a people born of God. They would be truly God's. They would be His products, His new creation, His glory. And offered up in the life-giving hands of His only-begotten Son, they would be acceptable to Him, and He would be glorified in them.

That's what happened to you. A real rebirth. A reconstituting of the root principles upon which and out of which you build your life. A new source, center, and network of origins. It means changed expression, a new style of produced life, truthful witness in harmony with God's true nature and way of dealing with the world and with men. It means, for this new people of God, a new kind and volume of wealth. For when Jesus Christ suffered death to take up a position of centrality in our lives, when He assumed our guilt in order to transform the very centers of our beings, He claimed those reclaimed lives as His very own. And having received us into His tradition of service and outgoing love, He was then able finally to offer to His Father what in fact belonged to Him. You were there when He elevated the offering of a people before His Father and said: "All Mine are Thine, and Thine are Mine, and I am glorified in them."

Our glory, our wealth is centered in the Christ in us. That's where it all comes from. He is the new Origin and Generator of the products, effects, expression of our lives, the driving life principle producing the objects and actions of our wealth. For house and home and car and children and health and sky and water .and life I continually give thanks. In prayer I daily return to Him with thanksgiving and praise all my loved ones, glorifying Him for their loan to me for the day in which I enjoyed them. In speech and action and attitude and behavior I draw upon the resources of that One who lives within me, and I move with the untroubled assurance that the witness of my life reflects the truth about my Maker and Redeemer. I rejoice in the profound opportunity to present my body as a living sacrifice, holy and acceptable to God through His Son, and praise Him for the privilege of sharing in His glory.

Someone has said that all of life — all creation, all of history and mankind — are like the elements of a tremendous sacrifice in the process of being consecrated. It's as if we and all things were caught up in that moment in which the High Priest elevates the priceless gift before the King and then lays it at His feet — the supreme and ultimate act of giving glory to the Most High God.

Tonight, as in every moment of your lifetime, Jesus Christ presents you to His Father as an offering, along with an unnumbered host of others whose lives and destiny are inseparably bound to His own. As He offers you to the King, He says: "All Mine are Thine, and Thine are Mine, and I am glorified in them."

Security

I do not pray that Thou shouldst take them out of the world but that Thou shouldst keep them from the evil one.

John 17:15

People today are confused. They really don't know what to do. There are too many unknowns, too many complicating qualifications, too many ambiguities, too many problems and paradoxes. The world is no longer a simple place to live, work, and raise a family. We are definitely becoming more crowded.

Along with this, the byword is *change,* with virtually every group and institution, from the family to whole governments, undergoing one form of revolution or another. Industries that purred along for a hundred years now find they must radically overhaul their philosophy and retool their entire mode of operation if they hope to survive. Pollution poses a whole spectrum of major worldwide threats. Moral systems are breaking down, with new and strangely different ones taking their place. Decadence, violence, profiteering, and a growing attitude of "every man for himself" seem to overwhelm valiant efforts on the part of some to generate countertrends, stopgaps, and hopeful reversals that may still salvage for another generation some fragments of the good, the pure, and the beautiful.

The first portion of Jesus' prayer in our thoughts tonight must come as a mild disappointment to some of us. Life, after all, is not easy. You get tired. After so much struggle, hard work, and the draining, ceaseless concerns of years and years, you quite naturally feel justified in looking around for peace, for some rest, for a chance to enjoy the fruit of so much consistent and long-rang output. For many, however, sickness, family trouble, economic reversal, or social change has wiped out that life's dream. And if that has ever happened to you, if your survey of life's current scene moves you to say, "I'm glad I'm on my way out," or if you're one of those who sit perspiring in stacked-up summer traffic listening to some grim 5:30 newscast, dreaming wistfully about the coral sands and azure skies of some remote South Sea island, then you too might wish on occasion that when Jesus left to go to His Father, He had also taken *you* along.

But that's simply not the way things are. We cannot escape. We are here — called to live with purpose within a context that is clearly infected by the presence of evil. Like a school of fish under attack by large predators, which leap out of the water and into the air — as if to find safety in another foreign environment — only to fall back to where the terror, the death, the flight, and the battle really are, so it is fruitless for us to flee from what is. No high fence, no disengaging distance in this fast-shrinking world, no "philosophical avoidance," monastic mountain retreat, or drug-induced cop-out can provide safe immunity from the negative powers constantly around and within us. For we are not only the *victims* of evil's manifestation in the world; we, along with all other men, are its hapless *bearers* and share in its processes and effects. Wherever people are, there it is; and no humanly devised inner or outer defense is adequate to shield us from it. To play the ostrich is foolish, could be fatal. We are *in this world* as it is and therefore in critical contact with all its realities. It only remains to be seen what we shall do about that contact and with those realities. Like touching a hot stove.

It is precisely at this point that the purpose underlying this petition of our Lord's High-Priestly prayer begins to become apparent. We should remember that He prays specifically for *us* when we hear Him say: "I do not pray that Thou shouldst take them out of the world but that Thou shouldst keep them from the evil one."

There is a reason. Who more than God does not desire that He be united fully and finally with His people? Who more than God's own Son? Why should He leave them behind in a life of complex and insoluble difficulty, to live through all the ache, the pain, the constant threat and unrelenting demand, when He Himself has bred into Christians everywhere that deep restlessness that finds its cure only in an ultimate security and rest in the bosom of God Himself?

The fact is that God wants us here. And He wants us to be here as we are — as people with one foot on earth and one foot in heaven. For our baptism into Christ Jesus was worked by God that we should be partakers of the same nature and experience of the God-man, Jesus Christ:

- that the hulls of these bodies should also be bearers of His life and Spirit.
- that our true humanity be blended with God-ordained apostolicity.
- that our realistic estimate of evil coexist with an equally realistic appraisal of the power of God to conquer it.
- that our presence provide a signal — like light that shines in darkness — of that "nevertheless" presence of God in the midst of a world that seems so hopelessly confounded.

"*In* this world and yet not *of* it," as we say. And this describes the set and stance of a people unique and precious to God, sent into *this* world — *our* world — to do a job for Him. This is no mean task. For the necessity of living a double life — as both citizen of the world and agent of God's kingdom — involves substantial risk. In an age of radical imbalance, of change, paradox, and fluctuating values, the maintenance of a posture that reflects both sensitivity to the realities and needs of the world and faithful commitment to our mission as God's people is by no means simple.

Survival alone as a Christian is not simple. For when Jesus prays to His Father, "that Thou shouldst keep them from the evil one," He prays in dead seriousness. He calls on God to "take over" in the rescue of those for whom He lays down His life.

For Satan is no slouch. He is that great, brooding, and powerful unholy spirit whose dominion permeates this entire created order. To think any man could stand before him to defy him or to outflank his strategies and wisdom is at best sheer madness, at worst an incredible foolishness. Satan is an *angel,* king of the kingdom of darkness, grand puppeteer who manipulates the dance of his subjects by the stringworks of a varied program of evil. And tragically, chief among the elements of his character is his distinction as the supreme liar. His lie always meets the ready inclination of our flesh. His lie is, "Don't get uptight — everything is okay." And when Christians buy it, they inevitably forfeit their special vocational stance, their vision, their courage. In short, they — in one way or another — lose their Christian balance.

For it is Satan who fosters the sense of confidence with which Christians make peace with the world — to the degree that they become indistinguishable from unbelievers.

It is Satan who lulls Christians into compromising the Gospel by silence or half-truth — when the reality of the human condition calls for utter clarity and direct communication of the truth.

It is Satan who "delivers" Christians from the pain of crisis and rejection that always accompanies confronting the world with the Gospel — and habituates them to a satisfaction with the practice of skirting issues with innocuous and inadequate words and actions.

Buying the lie is also the prelude to a loss of vision. We may grow to actually hate the world, justifying the abandonment of our mission to it with rationalizations that appear to be perfectly logical when viewed in the light of contemporary conditions.

"What's the use?" "Leave it to the experts," "Oh, for the good old days!" Or: "I've done my share; now let someone else do theirs." All these are in one way or another a common form of retreat from life into the gravelike security of the "wishing world" — the world

26

of disengagement and nonmission, noninvolvement with the realities of the here and now. And the wool-puller is the enemy, the liar, the evil one, Satan, the one from whose power our Lord prays to the Father for our deliverance.

On that night in the Upper Room, Jesus could pray with confidence that we remain at our posts in the world. He could because He trusted the Father, who sent Him on *His* mission to the world. He trusted God to see Him through death and into the victory of His exaltation. For in a short while the praying Christ would become the crucified Christ — whose work on Calvary freed us from the evil one and bared him as liar, wrenched open the grip of Satan on the world, and snapped the spine of his power over the lives and affairs of men.

It is this exalted Christ who is able to say, "I have overcome the world." It is this Christ, raised from the dead to rule the world jointly with the Father, who sends us into it to function as leaven and witness, who is "by our side upon the plain with His good gifts and Spirit."

That Spirit also strengthens us. He gives the vision to see through the last feeble attempts of a beaten Satan to enlist our allegiances. He gives perception and balance — to see through the victimizing influences of evil to the people who suffer under its yoke. He gives courage to face the distortions, the discouragements, and the hectic chaos of the 20th-century condition and to see God still at work in the world with His enduring "nevertheless." He leads us into the truth that those who live and die in Christ do so in the victorious confidence that we are involved in a cause and process that moves through tribulation to an ultimate and unimpeachable victory in the very near future.

And so, at this third stopping point on our "Journey to Joy" and as we put our hand to the difficult, glorious task of mission, our hearts leap in full and confident thanksgiving as we hear our Savior say: "I do not pray that Thou shouldst take them out of the world but that Thou shouldst keep them from the evil one."

Truth

Sanctify them through Thy truth. Thy Word is truth.

John 17:17

That must have been a spectacle. It was as if a pall of false-hood had suddenly dropped down to cover the entire situation, along with everybody in it. Or like the movement of plague, which quietly infects a whole population without anyone being aware of it. The religious leaders of Jerusalem had contrived a plot that was based on a whole system of fabrication. Pilate stooped to lie, compromising both himself and his position as governor. Witnesses, brought up to testify against Jesus, lied. Judas jigs to the rhythms of the death dance, contributing his share in the forms of crude betrayal and deceit. Peter, afraid for his own safety, blurts out, "I do not know the Man!" And the disciples, forgetting their recent, death-defying confession at Caesarea Philippi, now scramble with fear, crashing through the underbrush of a local garden in the wide-eyed panic of escape.

And when you let your eye drift slowly across the whole scene of the Passion, it seems that the only one there who is really telling the truth and *being* true is our Lord Himself.

Talk is cheap. And it seems to be getting cheaper all the time. Words. They pour out of our radios and TV sets. Visually they assault us from billboards, storefronts, newspapers, magazines. The libraries and research depositories of our age store them by the ton. Words. They are written, printed, spoken. Painted, filmed, micro-filmed. Reproduced, computerized, enlarged, symbolized. Many peo-

29

ple say there are simply too many of them, that they "go in one ear and out the other," that they "bounce off" without even beginning to register. Psychologists tell us that we have taught ourselves to shut many of them out by the cultivation of a "selective deafness."

But of equal importance to us tonight is that some are beginning to say, "Words have lost their value, and we are outgrowing them." They have lost some of their power. They no longer move people the way they used to. We have learned too that ads don't always tell the truth, and we arm ourselves behind a subtle, quiet skepticism. Lawlessness, they say, is the renunciation of principles that are largely rooted in the verbal orientations of people, that lawlessness stems from the separation of a person from insights that develop out of the long-term absorption of meanings and concepts shaped by words. The almost-daily appearance of cartoons in our newspapers about speech-making senators, who may be "phogbound" but are never at a loss for words, is a subtle form of black humor commenting on the failing American trust in political words and their power. And the disdain of contemporary youth for bloated and meaningless rhetoric bristles with repeated demands from the ranks of the young to "tell it like it is."

Well, tonight's prayer of Jesus to His Father was for us. And for this world too. But I think it's going to be a *hard* prayer for a world that has gotten around to distrusting and perhaps devaluing words. Listen to these words, and judge for yourself: "Sanctify them through Thy truth. Thy Word is truth."

It's true. Fulfillment of this petition depends completely on the word "Word." If God wants to sanctify anyone, He's going to have to send words into the world. It will depend on His Word, His words, even in a world that's stuffed and gagging on words.

Because of our deep involvement in our culture and our quite normal participation in its characteristic features, even we as Christians tend to operate with a minimal estimate of words. To us too, *all* words seem temporary, fragile, fleeting, mere servants in the communication of ideas, sounds that are born in our throats and then quickly die "out there," in the air, evaporating to nothing, in nothing. At best, some may persuade, but most are of use only for the moment — instruments for the purposes of common thought.

But have you ever wondered why, after all the instruction given them, the church generally loses a substantial number of its postconfirmation youngsters? Or have you ever wondered why there seems to be such a gap between where the church *is* today and where so many people say it *should* be? How could it be that the cream of Israel's ecclesiastical hierarchy, the disciples, competent scribes, learned Pharisees could participate in the abandonment of Jesus Christ to death by crucifixion? Have you ever personally struggled with the difference in yourself between *knowing how you are* and *being what you are* as a child of God? That it's by no means "easy" to move from Point A to Point B spiritually, because *knowing* what's got to be done can never somehow bring off the *doing* of it?

A vital step in the Christian's "Journey to Joy" has to do with this question. And a vital approach — and solution — to the problem is present in Jesus' affirmation to His Father, "Thy Word is truth."

In Jesus' day "word" involved a concept quite different from ours. The terms "word" or "words" meant considerably more to the people of Biblical times than they do to us today. Words were thought of as concrete things, as things that were alive. They were more than compressed air waves or combinations of vibrations that made audible and intellectual sense. Words — and especially the Word of God — were revered, even feared, as living things, with their own built-in energy and life.

Furthermore, because they were alive, they were instruments of action. They had power to perform. For once it was uttered, a word of God moved out into the mainstreams of time, into the midst of the people to whom it was addressed. And at a moment designated by God, out of the pressure of its own self-contained life, it would inevitably come to truth — to the full realization of its meaning in the everyday life and experience of the people for whom it was spoken. This "functional" characteristic of God's Word has a profound significance for all men. For when His Word "blooms" in their midst, its "fulfillment in fact" stands among men as a new and inescapable reality, irrespective of the human acceptance or rejection of it.

Thus God's Word does not "return to Him void." His words are never "wasted." They do not "bounce off" people and situations or fade to nothing in thin air. His Word is the word of a *faithful* God. It accomplishes the purposes for which it was delivered. It is a *living* Word, a Word that acts. It comes to truth.

And thus for our Lord to pray, "Thy Word is truth," is for Jesus to affirm that His Father's counsel and will for the world will inevitably prevail. Like seed cast by a sower, like tares and wheat sown in the same field, like the planting of a mustard seed and grain that germinates secretly in the night, as surely as harvest follows planting, the promises and intentions of God for the world will come to tangible birth among men. That's why God, when the fullness of time had come and His Son was to be born, sent an angel with His Word that His name should be called "Jesus," for He would in fact "save His people from their sins." That's why, when God, who at sundry times and in diverse manners spoke to men of old through His prophets — when God determined in these latter days to speak His ultimate and most powerful Word to the world through a *Son,* His Word was made *flesh* and dwelt among us in the person of Jesus Christ, the Way, the Truth, the Life. God's Word is truth. God's Word is Jesus Christ. God's truth is His Son.

Each one of us tonight — for that matter, any Christian anywhere — is a living example of God's Word come to truth. For somewhere in the history of each one of us a decisive word was spoken that flowered into meaning and transforming effect in our lives. Perhaps for you it was in Holy Baptism, "for it is not the *water* of Baptism that does such great things but the word of God which is in and with the water." Perhaps it was some word of

God like, "God will have all men to be saved and to come unto the knowledge of the truth" — and that will become operative and alive in you. Perhaps it was the coalescence of a number of words of God, each contributing to a comprehensive impression of God's love, peace, forgiveness, and protection in Christ for you. However it may have been, each one of us who bears the name of Christ is among all those of us who have been called by God's truthful Word into a relationship with Him through Jesus Christ — to *be* and to *live* in a way that is unique and set apart.

Because that's what His Word does. It sets us apart for His sacred purposes. For when God's Word comes to truth in the people to whom it is sent, then they are sanctified through that truth, they are set aside and ordained for the central reconciling and saving purposes of God Himself. It is through the birth of God's truth in us, through the planting of the reality of the living, indwelling Christ at the center of our lives, that we now become that missionary people that shows forth the praises of Him who has called us out of darkness into His marvelous light.

People who live the "sanctified life" tend to grow. The "words of God" keep coming to truth in them. Whole attitude systems are transformed. In one way or another they keep moving toward a kind of completeness. Their concern for one another and for others begins to emerge. They find ways to overcome problems, hindrances, frustrations, divisions. Their love grows. Personally they become convinced and sure of things — not in an opinionated or intolerant way — but their confidence and assurances are linked to realities. They never seem to be out of touch with the truth in situations. Whatever they seem to think, say, or do usually always winds up meaning something, or being something, good. Helpful. Positive. Reconciling. They come to "be like" the transforming Christ within them. And most important, I suppose, is that they keep talking to one another, in a thousand different ways, the many words of God by which they find themselves a people in whom those many words keep right on blossoming out into reality among them and in them. Thus sanctification is not only a stance or status or condition but a continually emerging, fulfilling way of life.

What should all this mean for us?

They say that a person who tells the truth never has to remember what he said. The idea is that he doesn't need to live with the haunting fear of being found out. He isn't under the bondage of the first lie, which forces him to "cover" with more of the same. Rather he can move with confidence. Because he is true, he tells the truth and enjoys the "moral ease" that results from being that way. In other words, he's *free.*

Jesus told the people He sanctified, "You shall know the truth, and the truth shall make you free." To His followers He promised the Holy Spirit, the Spirit of Truth, who was sent to "lead them into all truth."

This means that you can relax. God is no remote, uncompromising "boss" with an unblinking eye but a truly loving, caring Father. The Bible is not a "code book for religious living" but a means by which God bears witness to the sanctifying work of the Word made flesh. Rather the central impulse and generating source of your Word-sanctified life is nothing less than the indwelling Christ Himself. And as His influence spreads throughout the areas and dimensions of your life — in other words, as more and more of His words come to truth in you — it will become more and more "natural" to live and think and speak and act as He did. You don't need a law or a rule to get you to conform to a "right way of being," because at the generative center out of which all your life flows is the Word of Truth: Jesus Christ. You can *trust* the motives, decisions, attitudes, objectives of your "sanctified self." You can relax.

Secondly, change need not alarm you. Since you are a person in whom God's words are continually coming true, change is no stranger to you. Nor is it a threat. We are always on the move anyhow, growing, maturing toward the full stature of our crucified and risen Lord. Thus we accept challenge with an assurance that is rooted in an accomplished victory and becomes the early messenger of upcoming horizons and new contexts within which we have the privilege to declare the truth of a gracious God. Problems become opportunities, negative circumstances become the carriers of hidden and constructive potentials and possibilities, and even our anxieties over "the difference between where I am and where I should be" are dissolved within an expectant "waiting upon God" that trusts Him to bring His Word for me to living, observable reality.

"Sanctify them through Thy truth. Thy Word is truth."

Love

I have declared unto them Thy name and will declare it, that the love wherewith Thou hast loved Me may be in them and I in them.

John 17:26

I dare say that if any of us here tonight were told that we had only a few weeks to live, we would immediately, as they say, go about "setting our affairs in order." We would wind things up at the place we work, settle our finances, provide for the disposition of our estate. We would try to get everything done that we later would be unable to do; and we would make sure that our death would cause the least possible inconvenience to those around us and close to us.

And when all that was taken care of, we'd certainly apply the same or more effort to the relational and personal dimensions of our lives. Friends would call. There would be some long-distance phone calls. Ordinary things, like mealtimes and evenings at home with the family, would take on a more than ordinary significance. We would gradually become aware of the very real place and distinctive tones of past, present, and future and of their individually unique contribution to our lives. There would be thoughtful, sensitive, and reminiscent conversations with relatives and close friends — probably in the form of small, quiet gatherings that lasted late into the night. There would be long walks with people who were always special to us, and probably thoughtful and nostalgic interludes with our children, especially the very young.

We would sense things we had not caught in an entire lifetime. We would think thoughts, make observations, and say things that under normal circumstances in a·whole lifetime might never come to birth in our hearts or on our lips. And it just might be that throughout it all we would experience the discovery of what a profoundly important place and role *love* has in our lives.

I say all this in an effort to hypothetically *reduce* our situation tonight in order that you might sense this basic truth — that when we pare life down to its essential elements and momentarily remove all the lesser things attached to it and cluttered around its core, we find that the most beautiful human energy and the deepest continuing need of our existence is that of love.

Love is that often sacrificial energy that rescues living and dying from an experience bounded by sheer biological mechanism and that plants wonder, personality, and tenderness in an otherwise systematic and largely predictable world.

Love is that inner quality of mutuality and special honor in which human beings may hold one another.

Love is the often tender, sometimes fierce, but always steady acknowledgment of the other's claim on us and of our claim on the other.

Love is the unobtrusively understood sharing of a common trust, a unity of esteem.

For I would venture to say that that esteem — that meaning of the other — the touch and presence of the loved one — by far outweighs all other cherished values in our lives. For in the countless, everyday experiences of people everywhere, and perhaps especially in experiences that in some way are extreme or bittersweet people instinctively turn to those whom they hold dear for the hope, comfort, and assurance that can be found among men only in the love of and for the beloved. And it's true.

It was clearly evident in the boxcars and deathcamps of Nazi Germany and in the shelters, subways, and cellars of almost all of Europe a generation ago. It is so among the fatherless families of our ghettos and the homeless victims of Vietnam. It has always been so — from the dreadful child-labor mines and the begrimed huts of long-forgotten factory towns, in the shacks of sharecroppers and the cabins of the Appalachian backlands. In our day too in the homes of the rich and the hovels of the poor among the great and the humble, the exceptional and the average. It's peculiar to love alone that when the chips are down, men will somehow find it in themselves to care. They will sacrifice, give of themselves, even die for the sake of the one or the ones they love. It is true.

In our day psychiatric and counseling services, sensitivity and therapy groups, and a growing number and variety of structured settings in which people search for some inner sense of peace and worth and acceptance, all testify to the desperate and universal craving for that one, critical determinant of the ability of people to live happily and successfully with others, with themselves, and with the rest of the world. It's as if the one huge and comprehending need of our persons, relational experiences, our courts and inner cities, our families, our labor-management problems, and our economic, diplomatic, and international relations — all pointed to that one thing which after all is said and done is really the only thing on earth that makes living hre worthwhile. And that is love.

We have found that parentless babies in public institutions, otherwise normal and physically healthy, simply stop living or growing or only slowly and retardedly grow — for lack of the warmth, the caressing touch and fondling, the words and the sounds and the cares of love. Orphanges, hospitals, institutions for the aged, prisons — even sometimes families — are frequently the pitifully and inevitably destructive settings in which somehow there just isn't enough love to go around.

We are always, it seems, somehow out of balance. For quite a while now the expression has been, *"Show* me that you love me." *"Actions* speak louder than words." But really, now — in the endearing and intimate communications of lovers — could you ever imagine a romance without words? Isn't all of married life a series of both *actions* and words which in one way or another indicate the shared trust and effort of two people to pursue the objectives of life together? That is what love is all about, indeed. We develop attitudes — inner systems of feeling about ourselves and others that find expression in a wide variety of ways — on the basis of not only our interaction with people but also by way of verbal exchange. And it is even possible to say that actions are given, received, and shared in on the basis of verbal understandings and interpretations that group themselves in and around the people involved. Our actions may indeed speak loudly, but they never outgrow their need for the interpreting word.

That's why no love affair is ever totally silent. The words reflect the actions of the lovers, and their actions are reflective of their words. He calls her "darling" or "beloved," and she *believes* him because his eyes, his actions, his regard for her all "say" the same thing.

Love is really crippled without two legs to stand on. For its realization and growth it needs confession, articulation, interpretation, and explanation. For what we say and manifest toward people really adds up to "calling them by a name." They come to know themselves as we think of them. By our words and actions we tell them what or who we think they are — the regard in which we hold them. This is the way the "images" of ourselves and others are shaped. For no one simply is the way he always was. You constantly *find out* who you are and how you are from the "impress" of others on you. It's like getting a name, like constantly being named something, and then reflecting that name through the living of your life — the expression of who you really believe yourself to be. Tell a girl she's beautiful long enough, and she'll *become* just that. On the other hand, call a boy "hood" or "punk" long enough and consistently enough, and he'll come to believe that name, and that's exactly what he'll be.

And so you can see that there is a real connection between the way we feel about people and how they sense our feelings about them. And you can see too that whether they think of words or not, they receive names from us — and those names have an influence in the way they think about themselves and will therefore somehow find expression in their lives. If this is so, then you can immediately see how important it is that people be named with the words of love.

In the "utterly reduced" situation of the eve of His death and with all the ache and strain of His Savior's heart, Jesus beseeches His Father to create in us the same sustaining love which He experienced in His relationship with Him. He says:

"I have declared unto them Thy name and will declare it, that the love wherewith Thou hast loved Me may be in them and I in them."

He used to be named Smith or Miller or Carpenter because that was what he *did*. Or they called him Cartwright or Peterson or Paynter or Weaver because that's what he *was* in the town — he was what he did.

Jesus' words, "I have declared unto them Thy name," was not a simple statement. For the "name" in Jesus' day was not just a "handle," a convenient means of identifying specific persons. No, the name was intimately related to the nature of its bearer. When a Jewish father named his son, that name — a word — had a *meaning*. It was not a meaning that simply reflected the pride or joy of the father or even a hope that moved in the father's heart. It was rather the *certainty* that the name laid on the son — a word — would come to truth in the actual life of the boy and that the record of the boy's existence would be a fulfillment of the meaning of his name. Thus, when a Jewish father called his son Ben-jamin, he expected that the "son of the right hand" would be the one who would always stand as protector, as powerful "right-hand-man" of the father. And if a father chose to call his son Joa-chanan (John), he lived with the certainty that the life of that child would actually demonstrate that "Jehovah is gracious."

In Old Testament thinking and in that of our text, the name itself *is* the person, it is so closely related to the nature of its bearer. That's why they called His name "Je-sus" -- because it was understood that one so named would demonstrate with His life that

"Jehovah saves" — that the meaning of the name laid upon Him would emerge as the factual, actual demonstration of His life.

Jesus in His words and His acts, in His very living and being declared the name of God. He was God's fullest, most descriptive, most complementing word — the word made Flesh. "No man has seen God at any time; the only-begotten Son, who is in the bosom of the Father," He has represented, described, manifested Him. This means that Jesus was the One who in the expression of His life and in His words was God's name lived out for us. Jesus translated *God* into words and actions and in so doing declared God's name, testified to God's person, to His attitudes and feelings toward us. He impressed upon us by word and action, by the very nature of and meaning of His person and word, the way God is and so became the demonstration of the reality of God's stance in relation to us.

And this all comes out to say one thing, one word: love. This is what God is. And this is what He wants us to be also as His children.

How embarrassing! Again we experience the distance between where God would have us and where we really are or know ourselves to be. For when we think about it, frequently our loving of other people hardly seems authentic at all. We have loved with such a poor record, so self-consciously and inconsistently, so artifically and even egocentrically, that we blush to think that Jesus speaks about *us* when He prays, "that the love wherewith Thou hast loved Me may be in them and I in them." In effect this statement implies that *love* ("what the world has too little of") must come from· the church, in and through its relation to God with Christ, for this is the only way He can adequately be represented in the world. For God intends that the Christian's love be an extension and continuation of His own.

I must confess that I know my love to be bogged down, crippled, and clogged with all kinds of ambiguity, with apathy, selectiveness, and self-interest. At best we seem always to be operating with divided hearts — never really possessed by a love within us but always qualifying, considering, compromising, neutralizing.

But the real test comes every time we are given opportunity to live as extensions of God's love. For that love moves calmly and persistently and with purposeful care and intelligence in the face of resistance, rejection, and even hate. It sets no limits to its intensity or endurance. It cares *before* caring is "the appropriate thing" to do; and it is willing to be hurt in order to bring healing. And in, with, and under the attitude that never expects a reward it moves with the motives of forgiving.

That's the way God plans for us to go about calling people names and helping them to shape images about themselves. That's the instrument, the name-giving of love, through which He longs to have people come to an inner belief of who they are and thereafter to live with one another as people who were loved with the intent that they also would be able to love.

My dear Christian, if you are sincerely concerned about the divine dimensions of love as healing, enriching, and effective motions in your life; if you are at all moved in your heart to want the fulfillment of Jesus' prayer to begin to shape and energize your living; if the inner conviction about your own capacities for actively and honestly loving has wearied and worn thin through unfulfilled resolutions and frustrated trials and left you at the point of resignation and neutrality; if you find yourself tied up and confused with all kinds of stifling hesitations; then permit me the privilege of sharing with you some profoundly important counsel:

No man has ever seen God. No one ever spoke to Him face to face. No one could ever know His full name, because they never really knew Him fully. And so, in order that all this might be changed, He caused His own Son to be born a man. A *man,* so that He might be one of us, who were originally in God's image. *His* Son, so that He might be God, of the same divine nature as His Father.

Only thus could God's own beloved Son come to do our dying

for us. That death for us was incredible in its meaning, terror, and totality. But it was exacted precisely because you and I in our being, in our speaking, and in our doing *fail* to equal the loving of God Himself. That willing and substitutionary act of Jesus demonstrated to all men the profound extent of the love of God for us. The point is, that He loves us *as we are*. He meets and greets us with His patient and unselfish love *as* a people with crippled resources for loving and with our shortness of endurance. Our poor love, our ambiguous, fractured loving, and our abundant unloveliness did not frustrate His will to gather us, redeem us, and make us the objects of the loving will of His Father.

"God so loved the *world* that He gave His only-begotten Son that whosoever believeth in Him should not perish but have everlasting life." And He so loved His *Son* that on the third day, when the work of His death for us was accomplished, He raised Him up to give Him a place of everlasting Lordship and glory.

To everyone who is born of water and the Spirit, in the *name* of the Father, the Son, and the Holy Ghost; to everyone who believes in the *name* of the Word made flesh, God gives power to become one of His sons. To everyone who has been reborn, not of biological process alone but through the demonstration and witness of God's person in Jesus Christ has been born of *God* — to him God has given the name of *son*.

That rebirth has profound implications for us. It means that through Christ God the Father has laid His name upon us. It means that a new genetic system — a new heredity — now dominates within the substance of our persons. We have been called by a new name, the name of our new Father, laid upon us, declared to us by Jesus Christ. I am a sharer in a new heredity through a deathless word that has come to truth in me, declared by Jesus Christ our Lord! That's how the prayer of Jesus is fulfilled. That's how the Father answers the petition of a Son, who calls up out of the radically reduced situation of the eve of His own death. That's why you and I can be the living, loving objects and fulfillments of

44

the prayer: "I have declared unto them Thy name and will declare it, that the love wherewith Thou hast loved Me may be in them and I in them."

Life

This is life eternal, that they might know Thee the only true God, and Jesus Christ, whom Thou hast sent.

John 17:3

God really deserves more glory than He gets. I say this because life is so inexhaustibly marvelous. Try it out on yourself. Try to think of yourself as a precreation, prelife being; and then try to think of what it would be like to even conceive of a thing like life. Its creation was a brilliant stroke of the creative intelligence and goodness of God.

It is the central gift and blessing of our existence and of that of the rest of the world. And its uniqueness, I feel, resides in the fact that it goes on. It reproduces itself, extends itself relentlessly. Or, I guess — to think of it in another way — life has not only its immediate self but the prospect of an unpredictable number of other selves beyond it.

In a very basic sense life is free, open. It lives by growing. By its very nature it carries a promise about tomorrow. And its presence always implies expanding, multiplying possibilities, so that to say "hope" is really to say "life," because it means plurality, range of option, choice. More than today. More than now. More than what is.

Think of the grand, supportive context into which it has been placed. Water, seeking its own levels, fills the dry beds, erodes huge mountains into rich, alluvial plains, courses with brute and beautiful strength through subterranean vents and siphons. Sky and air — pressed in silent service to the bosom of life's arena — facilitate the secret and invisible exchanges that support its motion and its breathing. Moving within the rhythmic alternation of each day's dawn and sunset, geared to the pulse and alternation of productivity and rest, hung between the balances of quietly circling stars and the mute, mysterious flight of whole galaxies — cradled in all this are the dynamics of replenishment and fertility, the seasons of productivity and rest, the cycles of the restoration of expended power, and the ceaseless reproduction of life.

This is our home, where we share with all things in the benefits of God's profound and beautiful gift of life. Where children laugh and where babies are born, where men and women work and care and laugh and cry and tear down and build, where lovers shape their secret miracles and adorn the world with their joy, and where ancient men with wise words on their lips go down to honorable graves. This is our home where we live. It is all that we know. It is our life.

But if you take a second look, I'm sure you'll come up with the uneasy feeling that all this somehow doesn't tell the whole truth. It's as if there's a lurking sense of incompleteneses in it all. And there is. Because you can't only talk about life *quantitatively*. Life is qualitative too. Life is more than simply a matter of "how much" but also of "what kind" and "in what way" and "why." To live life in terms of its material and biological content alone is similar to the position a madman takes when he *rejects* whole dimensions of reality and operates as if they didn't even exist at all. Life is a matter of kind as well as degree. And as we've said, *limitation* is just not *in* life's character. Life is free. It should grow, expand, multiply.

It's all in the way we're built. As sinners all men are the inheritors and carriers of death. Not death of a "one shot" kind but rather a type of death that's loose in the world to constrict and impoverish all forms of human life, even while men live. It employs a subtle strategy. It caters to what it finds within the susceptibilities of people, and so the principle that's operative on the outside "shakes hands" with the sin-given readiness on the inside to hold a man in the grip of an enduring bondage.

Let me tell you what I mean. Because they live in an imperfect, fallen world, men live with all sorts of fears. So do we. We fear the unknowns of the future, and for security's sake, and with all sorts of work, financing, and planning, we pour our lives into fortifying ourselves against it.

We fear the threats of the present. Where they rise up suddenly before us, we react like men who become transfixed and immobilized at the sight of some charging beast. But a means of dealing with even this has taken shape of late. For thousands of people, "doing your own thing" has come to mean "licensed disengagement" from the claims of the present, the adoption of a personally selected and self-established system of response-monitoring, that enables one to "take it or leave it," depending on what the crisis might involve. This reincarnation of an obsolete American individualism enables people to outwardly function with a vogueish "here and now" attitude but in reality only masks the same tired, human readiness to maintain an egocentric security. And since the involvement of so many people in some of the crucial issues awaiting solution in corporate life today is determined on the basis of highly individual whims and value standards, it is easy to see why in so many dimensions of societal life we are in such deep trouble.

Others, like hurricane victims clinging to telephone poles and wind-shredded trees, respond to immediate challenges and needs by embracing and holding fast to "safe" things — "centers" around which they organize their lives. They lash themselves to the masts of financial stockpiling, to the pleasure principle of "get what you can while you can get it," or to the tired old game of status-building. But when the real challenges of life get too close, like race, social and community responsibility, war, drugs, the rearing of the modern young, or things like poverty, the meanings of religion and faith for life, and commitment to real people in real needs — when these become *frontal realities* for people whose lives are organized around such "security centers," then invariably reactions follow the usual pattern of confusion, fear, retreat, a hasty search for the comfort of familiar patterns, and the security of yesterday's status quo.

For people who fear the present, the stimulating risks to life in the here and now can be overwhelming, immobilizing. Rather than *commit* themselves without specific certainties, they *exit* themselves in search of them, backing out of the present and permitting themselves to be carried back into the safe prisons of the past. That is the price we pay for disengagement from the present — retreat from life into the four-cornered receptacles of the past.

But then there are those who live in the past. And for them the past is no safe haven. Rather the reference point that controls their present and future is an untouchable, unreachable tyrant, who rules from the irretrievable worlds of their yesterdays. These are the most pitiful — the scarred and unhealed products of crippled backgrounds and misshapen childhoods, the unrestored, living shambles of broken homes and marriages, the zombielike introverted unknowns who with deeply etched inferiorities and deeply rooted fears get through life only by dint of utter determination and the massive expenditure of effort. The dominating past is also the "center" of life for the guilt-laden and self-accusing — for the ones who live through nightly whisperings of memories and consciences that simply will not die — for the constantly compensating and the constantly counterfeiting, who in a thousand ways each day make apology or excuse or try to find justification for being alive at all — excuses and justifications which in their hearts they barely believe themselves. Shackled to the forces that shaped them in the past, they move in the present like men held captive by a length of chain that stretches behind them, anchored somewhere beyond the distant horizons of their past.

To be bound to the past is to be "out of it," and all who by choice or chance are fated to live in that shadowy realm are, in part at least, dead or dying. For when people choose the past or anything in it as their "safe center," they in reality choose *an idol.* For when we draw in the dimensions of living to hold us like a cradle and when we finally nestle down into the safe, solitary, simplicity of our refuge from life, it is only then — too late! — that we discover that refuge to be a *grave!*

Bondage to the past hinders growth, inhibits the freedom of life. Past-rooted fears prevent men from zestfully accepting the challenges and risks of the vital, incoming future. So in their preference for safety they find a place where the future cannot touch them. Choices are reduced. Life becomes monodimensional, solitary, and narrow and loses its expanding and reproductive character.

Evidences of this deadly principle are all around us: in the doctor who dares not stop but nervously drives past the carnage on the highway; in the citizen who leaves govenment to the "institution"; in the layman who leaves ministry to the pastor; in the pastor who leaves ministry to the "expert."

Also in all our lurking love of things on the earth: in all gracelessness and egocentricity; in all maneuver, manipulation, and domination by which we bludgeon the freedom and rightful expression of it in others; in every willful, thoughtless reduction of diversity or healthy individuality of others; and in every safe avoidance of the risk, adventure, and challenge to which God constantly calls us.

One of the greatest things about the Christian faith is that God loves so much that He is never unwilling to come to us. And not just once, mind you, but constantly, whether we think we need Him or not.

Jesus said, "I am come that they might have life and that they might have it more abundantly." He came that men might walk out of the mortuaries of their fears and into the bright, clean world of life — eternal life. And so He came to us. His mission was that we came to *know God* in terms of the experience of His presence in every part of our life. That "knowing" we call "to believe in Him as the only true God." And the revelation of that knowledge was made through the life, death, and resurrection of Jesus Christ. For it was through Jesus that God would call us out of the monodimensionality of choicelessness, out of the life-reducing tyranny of our fears — into the freedom of eternal life.

Before it can reproduce a harvest that is thirty-, sixty-, or one hundredfold, a kernel of wheat must be buried and die. Jesus was that Seed of the world's life who for us descended into the utter solitude of the grave and offered Himself as agent and representative of all mankind in suffering an absolute death. It fulfilled the justice of God's wrath against all of our idolatries, against every surrender of mission and responsibility in the face of fear, and against every responsibility we bore for the frustration and inhibition of life in the world and in the lifetimes of our fellowmen.

Furthermore, when we speak of God as "forgiving our sins" in Christ, we are speaking of a God who sets us free, who "leads us out of Egypt." Sin rules from the past. It reaches out of a bygone era to hold us in the present — to inhibit, deflate, and retard life in the here and now. That past influence weighs upon us so heavily in the present that it bottlenecks our resources and evaporates our confidence with respect to the steady stream of newness coming toward us from the future. When God *forgave* us in the cross and death of His Son, the bondage of the past was broken, freeing us for life in the present and making the incoming life of the future available to us. This is what St. Paul affirms when he says: "Therefore, if any man be in Christ, he is a new creature: old things are passed away; behold, all things are become new. And all things are of God, who hath reconciled us to Himself by Jesus Christ." (2 Cor. 5:17-18)

For Christians who live in the constant consciousness of their acceptance by God in Christ, each day is a new emergence into a stance and place where there is fertile newness and fullness of life — a newness and fullness that gives the vital power to transcend the narrowing dominions of imposed and self-bred stricture, that broadens perspective and stimulates an eager readiness for involvement in the teeming life of a new age. And this is life eternal, starting in the here and now with the experience of a forgiving God, through Jesus Christ, whom He has sent.

Thus the past is no longer to be feared. It is transformed by the redeeming presence of Him who is the same yesterday, today, and forever. The present, with all of its threats, becomes a context filled with opportunities and charged with the presence of that One who is with us always. The future need cause us no anxiety since that is the direction from which God comes and a portion of the life with which His life abounds. That's where He keeps coming from.

That's why it is truly meet, right, and salutary that we should at all times and in all places give thanks to Thee, O Lord, holy Father, almighty, everlasting God; and therefore with angels and archangels and with all the company of heaven to laud and magnify Thy glorious name, evermore praising Thee and saying, "Blessed is He who cometh in the name of the Lord."

Because God really deserves more glory than He gets — I say this because life is so inexhaustibly marvelous — try it out on yourself.

Joy

And now I come to Thee; and these things I speak in the world that they might have My joy fulfilled in themselves.

John 17:13

This is the morning of joy. It is a day of matchless happiness and wonder as the church on earth and in heaven echoes the shouts and songs of victory. It is a day on which the vaultings of eternity ring with the hosannas of angels and archangels and all the company of heaven. It is a day on which God crowns His Son with glory and honor and gives Him dominion over all things that have life and breath! The Son of Man, who traveled the road of sorrows and death, has emerged in the joy of victory to take His place at the right hand of God through a resurrection! He lives, never again to die. He is risen *from* the dead. All creation lays aside the sadness of death and joins in the lifting up of hearts, hands, and voices before Him who is our Risen Joy.

That's the only place it could have ended. Because all the milestones of our "Journey to Joy" registered both direction and promise. They all spoke of a present reality and future hope that could only add up to our utter and total joy. Like pilgrims who have traveled toward the brilliance of an Easter sunrise, each one of our steps through Lent has been more brightly lighted than the one that came before, by the dazzling goal before which we stand this morning — the tomb is vacant! He is risen as He said!

And that is God's signal of approval on everything for which His Son prayed:

For our present *unity* in Christ is but the preview of an eternal unity with God in *glory*. And our *security* here is but the prelude to our deathless security in the eternal presence of the Father! And the *truth* He works in us here prepares us for the glory of our completed fellowship with God in the fullness of the victorious Christ! And the *love* He has shown us in time is but the beginning of that incomparable grace that will endure forever. And the *life* He has granted, victorious over death, will be a life that never ends. He has spoken these things to us in the world, so that His joy, this joy He now knows, in having accomplished all He undertook to do, might be in us also.

Even now, today, the joy of Jesus is directly related to us. You should really think about that for a while. His joy is in the people whom He calls "His glory." With the same kind of exuberance, the same sense of accomplishment, with the same satisfying rewards of *completion* with which we rejoice in a job well done, so does Jesus, after His exaltation in cross and resurrection, "hurry home" with a full and delighted heart to rejoice with His Father over the complete and successful fulfillment of His redemptive task: "Well done, thou good and faithful servant!"

And there is nothing unreal or abstract about it. Because Jesus is now inseparable from us. I am part of His body. "He lives, my ever-living Head." Raised to a position of corulership with God the Father, He now governs all things with the central interest and design for our share in His eternal fullness and rulership, so that the full consummation of His prayer be granted — the prayer that goes: "Father, I will that they also, whom Thou hast given Me, be with Me where I am, that they may behold My glory, which Thou hast given Me."

All this, together with the joy He now experiences, stems from His completed work. For a people who sat in darkness and in the bondage of an unbreakable servitude to the *past* He came as deliverer, freeing them from the shrouds and chains of bygone sin and guilt and the dominion of a crumbling kingdom of darkness. He brought down the satanic power in shattered and final defeat, liberating them for life in the present vigor and challenge of the kingdom of God. He sanctified the past by taking up a redeeming position in the past of every Christian who by faith is able to call God "Father." This is His joy. Ours too.

Second, for a people cowed and fearful of the present He now corules with the Father over all things *in* the present — at this very moment — to assure them — holding every moment of our here and now in the sustaining security of His loving and unlimited power and control. Because of this, Christians everywhere are able to put their hands to the problems of the day and with full confidence of the Spirit's guidance, strength, and comfort *be* for the world as the embodied love and representatives of their Lord.

Third, because of the comprehensive control of the victorious Christ, the Christian's future is "sheltered." Everlasting life is for us a present reality, initiated in Holy Baptism and extending beyond death's comma into the limitless reaches of eternity. What's left to fear? With the future "coming in" from the hand of a gracious Lord whose love has been evident in so many ways and to such degree, who could be anything *but* joyous? We are an "Easter people," living constantly in the full knowledge of the resurrection and its implications for "yesterday, today, and tomorrow." Our Christ-centered life "sandwiches" the meaning of the future right up against the everyday realities and experiences of the present. And so we have joy — joy that spills over into life, that makes of life a resurrected worship *oriented to* a resurrected Lord.

But is that so? *Is* there the present evidence of a grip, a confident sense of victory, an assurance today about the "income" of tomorrow that characterizes daily Christian life and worship? Perhaps. But perhaps there should or could be more. Let us see.

Sometimes you'd think it wasn't true. Of course, it's all a matter of impression and observation, but among many Christians you'd think that their *hope* was only barely alive! With *resignation* they say, "Everything's in the Lord's hands. What will be will be" — as if that's all they know about it. Others say, "You've got to take it as it comes — you can't fight it." Or, "Well, that's the way it is" — as if the resurrection of Jesus Christ had nothing to *do* with the future!

Christians are even nervously "tuned out" with respect to the future, writing it off as unpredictable, as if there were nothing to count on, as if we were all *victims of it* rather then covictors *in it*. Others have low or no expectations. Neutral, they "leave the future alone," not trusting it, fearing that anticipations set too high are only setups for disappointment and reversal, and adopt a neutral position. Fearing that their joy might go unfulfilled, they regard the future with nervous indifference and neutrality, taking it to be at best something untouchable, at worst a potential, untrustworthy negative. Consequently conversations are joyless. Life for many is a bloody, sweat-soaked, uphill battle without any prospect of letup! Worship is *solely* a source of help, of the bottomless need for comfort, of the unquenchable quest for reassurance. Just to be. Just for today. Just to make it. Congregations full of Kyries. Crisis Communions. Somber suppers and years of dreary habit, sustained only by the constantly recurring need for a little more armor, for another week's reinforcement against the long, weary battle, for which I find surcease for one meager weekly hour in my Sunday morning pew.

Let me offer a suggestion. I guess life is so heavily mechanistic, perhaps even so full of predictable tensions and racing to keep up, that the future even holds little appeal.

Perhaps our problems are not in the area of our joy at all. Perhaps, before we can even consider joy, much less have it, we must deal with the matter of our Christian *hope*. Perhaps our joylessness — or our "uncultivated" joy — is only the *symptom* of an "uncultivated hope." For when our *hope* is full, then will our *joy* be also. Of this I am sure. Think of weddings. Or expecting babies. Or waiting for spring. Or getting ready for a date. Or being on your way downtown to pick up a new car. Or watching a crop growing in perfectly. Or seeing the beginnings of a sunrise. Joy shines with the promise of the *future*. Rejoicing happens when you depend, when you expect something good.

But let me tell you about the way some Christians live and, incidentally, how you might live also. First of all, to say that the Christian's postresurrection joy is one of uninterrupted and hilarious joy would simply not be true. All of life in our world is touched by the steady presence of sadness or at best by an intermittent sense of sadness. The most beautiful sunset or cloudscape will at first move you to feelings of awe and by the clash or softness of its coloration inspire deep movings of your inner spirit. But those same skies — while you watch them! — can also communicate a real but indescribable melancholy — a vacant, aching sadness that somehow makes contact, deep within us, with the knowledge of our transience, our fragility, and the ultimate passage and change of all things. The same holds true for those cherished memories and seasons of the past — cherished images of friends, vacations, the brief flashes of our remembered childhoods, and the glorious and profound events that every lifetime holds. But while they cause our hearts to warm and our faces to beam into minor smiles, they simultaneously convey their sense of the unrepeatable, of the sadly distant, and a sense of the cyclical, ongoing tyranny of time and the irretrievability of even the happiest moments of the past.

The truth is that the happy-sad ambiguity, omnipresent in all of life, is not changed into something else or wiped away forever by our Christian joy. Christians are not lifted by Baptism into a utopian never-never land of sustained and unrelenting hilarity. But rather a *new* and completely unique element of joy has been introduced into the patterns of their existence. Like an incarnation, the vertical dynamic of godly joy has intersected with all earthly ones, transforming them, enriching them. That vertical, "incoming" element is none other than the glorious, risen Christ. This is to say that such joy is rooted in the utter and unshakable assurance of the *positive* and *victorious* nature of the hope-giving future — the future out of which Christ reigns and from which He sends *only* such things as contribute toward our ultimate good. His gifts are both immediate and ongoing. He *gave* us unity, protection from evil, truth, love, life. But He still does so today and will *continue* to! Christ's joy is fulfilled when we, confessing Him as Keeper of our future, *trust* Him *in* that future. It is fulfilled in us when we, trusting ourselves to Him, receive with joy the good things He sends us from it.

Thus our joy is linked to the living hope of Christ's ongoing care for us and of that final and everlasting fellowship with Him toward which we daily move. Our consciousness of ourselves and of our place in time and space is all shaped by a threefold sense and security centered in the work of our Lord and Savior. Christ behind as Healer of the past, Christ present, risen, ruling victorious, Christ before, active in His control of all coming things for our sakes, daily readying new blessings to contribute to our joy. He, the grand Originator, Sustainer, and Concluder of all things, is the object of our hope and the source of all our joy. For true joy can issue only from the joy of a sure and certain hope. It not only exalts the spirit of the Christian and puts a smile on his face but has its influencing and shaping power in all the dimensions of his life. Such joy is creative. It moves toward an effect beyond itself alone. It has a purpose. It begins to show. It bears witness. It colors and gives unique substance to the Christian's dealings with other people. They come away from encounters with him somehow conscious of being the better for it. He stands out as a significant person because of an outlook or set of mind that is curiously and refreshingly free and infectious. Today, tomorrow, and yesterday, as anything else in life, never seem threatening or negative to him. There is something complete, whole, peacelike inside and about him. And when people meet and associate with him, they experience a tiny, preconscious curiosity, as if they were sure he had some rare and special insight or secret or as if he had knowledge of some otherwise unknown mystery.

He's also optimistic. He looks for the best. Problems are not only that but also challenges, opportunities. People are usually positive things for him, and when they don't turn up that way he's usually ready to put "the best construction" on things. He has confidence in people, and even when they fail his expectations, his positive regard and attitudes toward them seem to outweigh his disappointment in them. He forgives.

Then too he's a "yes" man. He'll be more inclined to discover things in his wife, among his children, among his co-workers and friends to *affirm* and to *praise* than to *criticize* or *condemn*. And he moves with an enviably secure and positive appraisal of himself as a valuable and significant child of God. He *really believes that God loves him.* And it shows in his life — a life that keeps on moving and accepting with joy whatever "comes in" from the future.

What this says is that joy becomes the vehicle of witness. Joy is essential to worship — the worship that is all of life, all of our behaving, all of the evidences of our being. When Jesus says, "And these things I speak in the world that they might have My joy," He is referring to His speaking, which goes on through Christians, who are His vocal and demonstrating representatives. For when His speakings are a way of life for Christians, not only is His joy fulfilled in *them,* but simultaneously the meaning of His death and resurrection is communicated to others. Witness is the overflow of joy, the key expression of the life of worship in Christ, the happy, un-self-conscious readiness of the child of God to "give an answer" with respect to the hope that is in him.

Well, how about you? Do you feel as if Christ's joy is fulfilled, completed, in your life? Is your life a joyful process of witnessing worship? Or would you say, "No, not yet. I've a long way to go"? Well, *His* joy *is* fulfilled in *you,* you know. You are His glory. You are His joy. *His* Lenten journey brought Him to *you.* Did your Lenten journey bring you to Him?

Though we struggle here through the ambiguities, the "ups and downs" of our sadnesses, and though our time here consists of alternating days of rain and sunshine, there nevertheless exists an absolute joy, the fixed and unchanging truth of our Lord's full and victorious joy, the sustaining underchord of joy in the certainty that all of life for us leads to the gracious heart of God.

It happens every year — it's as if God were underscoring His unbreakable word of promise, as if He were signaling to us out of the very tempos of earthly time. For every year, after the passage of winter's gray and discomforting barrenness, it happens. The crocuses and daffodils bloom. The forests and the meadows and the hillsides of the world move with an almost imperceptible trembling; and out of their gray-brown deadness there comes a miracle of surpassing wonder. They bloom again! The birds come back. The earth warms, breathes again with its intoxicating, life-giving breath. And the world once more is full of joy.